ECHOES

ECHOES

Poems Left Behind

By

John Ciardi

The University of Arkansas Press
Fayetteville   London   1989

Designer: Chiquita Babb
Typeface: Linotron 202 Ehrhardt
Typesetter: G & S Typesetters, Inc.
Printer: Thomson-Shore, Inc.
Binder: John H. Dekker & Sons, Inc.

The paper used in this publication meets the minimum require-
ments of the American National Standard for Permanence of Paper
for Printed Library Materials Z39.48-1984. ⊗

Library of Congress Cataloging-in-Publication Data

Ciardi, John, 1916–1986
    Echoes : poems left behind / by John Ciardi.
    p.   cm.
    ISBN 1-55728-062-2 (alk. paper).   ISBN 1-55728-063-0 (pbk. :
    alk. paper)
    I. Title.
PS3505.I27E25   1989
811'.52--dc19
                                        88-21927
                                            CIP

Contents

These are from among the poems of John Ciardi not included in any of the collections of his work published during his lifetime.

Nine of them have appeared in three volumes published since his death: "It is for the Waking Man to Tell His Dreams" in *John Ciardi: Measure of the Man,* edited by Vince Clemente; "Elegy for a Cove Full of Bones" in *Saipan: The War Diary of John Ciardi;* "A Love Poem," "In Species, Darling," "The Something/Nothing Any Love Can Tell," "I Was Not Sleeping nor Awake," "Darling," and "The Aging Lovers" in *Poems of Love and Marriage* by John Ciardi, all from The University of Arkansas Press. "A Trenta-Sei of the Pleasure We Take in the Early Death of Keats" appeared in *Patterns of Poetry: An Encyclopedia of Forms,* by Miller Williams, published by LSU Press. "Elegy for a Cove Full of Bones" appeared in the March 1988 issue of *Poetry.*

No one familiar with the work of John Ciardi will be surprised by his playful invention, in "A Trenta-Sei of the Pleasure We Take in the Early Death of Keats," of the word *psilanthropic* to mean "merely human," from the Greek *psilos* (mere) and *anthropos* (generic man). The trenta-sei as a form is also Ciardi's invention.

Special thanks to Betty Williams, whose almost unreckonable hours of reading, searching, and sorting have made her the most informed of anyone on the previously unpublished poems of John Ciardi, and made this volume possible.

ECHOES

One Easter Not on the Calendar I Woke

One Easter not on the calendar I woke
  and found I had survived ambition.
There was nothing I wanted more of. Time, yes,
  if it was given. An unfinished thought
to add a page to, not for the thought's sake,
  but for the pleasure of writing the page well,
if I could write it well. Or if not, for the trying.

My dog, having already outlived averages,
  sprawled at my feet, happy enough to breathe;
sometimes to raise a rabbit ten years dead
  and give chase, but wake foolish. When it happens
I give him a dog biscuit. There should be something
  after such dreaming. We sit and discuss
how fiercely the world ran the first of us. He knows
  there is always a second biscuit, waits for it,

then groans back to his rug and tries again
  for what can be raised from sleep. His habit is rabbits,
mine is pages. All night in the tomb
  the ghosts of pages walk—white revelations—
but when I wake still clutching the one I caught,
  it is always blank. I roll the stone away
and try to remember, and cannot, never enough.

But it is enough not to be back in the tomb.
  Come Easter one may try for no reason,

for the sake of trying. Because it is Easter.
    Because the sound of the old dog grinding biscuits
calls women singing to the well, and camels
    from the unspeakable sands, heavy with bales,
And bit by bit the page begins to fill.

A Man and a Woman
Might at This Moment

A man and a woman might at this moment,
in the complexities of rut, be begetting
a child, who in the gradual unevent
of journalistic history, by bed wetting

to patient training and a loving, slow instruction,
may some day read a poem and be changed
into himself in ways he could not have known
by reading the papers. This has been arranged

since the first glyph became an ancestral letter
and started to say a word. Or it took place
without arrangement, if random will do better
than the inevitable. In any case,

what that child does raising words from a page
to cadence and reverberation blows out
ministers, generals, and all the rage of passion
to waken a resonant place at the core of things.

Done for the Doing

Ape-handed, too bungle-knuckled
to hold a brush true
to the eye, and the image beyond it—

ham-fisted stumblier than any
instrument will sound
imagination from, or even feeling—

I am driven to scrawl words,
leaving printers to set
the spilled worms of my hand,

Sometimes I read what the printer did
and dare think, "yes," but don't
care. It's over by then.

This is for the doing. Done,
it's dead as the Chopin
my wife played years ago

and never went back to, though
a presence once. Like being.
And then, having been.

Love Sonnet:
Believing Part of Almost All I Say

It was a day that licked envelope flaps.
My hundred-roll of stamps solidified.
So much for communication. Is there perhaps
a self-improving technology? I tried
storing my writing things in the freezer (a tip
from the Anxiety Editor). All stuck
in a half-twist endless plane, a Moebius strip
flypaper logo of perpetual guck.

Since I was glued to my desk, I tried to write.
What might it not be like to have something to say?
In another continuum I stayed up all night
inventing a language I cannot read today.
But is time legible? I think of you.
No message. No medium. But still something to do.

Poetry

All poetry up to the present time
Has been a tribesman's venture into rhyme.

A praise of home, yes, but at heart a boast.
The animals of one valley, of one coast,

Of one belief—one people chosen right
To shine alone among the sons of might.

And if the tribesman wandered in exile,
That was his expiation, for a while.

A soul among the soulless, he was still
The braggart of one village on one hill

Unmatched by any Alp; and of one pond
Deeper than any seas that lay beyond

The call of fishermen in his one tongue.
However many lands he moved among

Odysseus lived at home, and Homer sang
To homefolks the glory of that gang

Of raiding roughies, and every clanging strophe
Meant only, "Folks, our boys have won the trophy!"

Freshman Sonnet: Success

Success in life is when one has a goal
and makes it. If, naturally, the goal is a good one.
Money is useful, but no man would alone
be successful just financially. Man has, also, a soul.
Therefore he should plan his life for more
than possessions, though they are a very fine thing.
To succeed, you should help the other fellow, and bring
a ray of cheer sometimes, and know what you stand for.

Success is to God, to country, and to community.
It is finding pleasure in giving pleasure.
It should also have diversity as well as unity.
Success is not one thing but it runs through life.
Success in marriage, for example, in large measure,
depends, of course, on getting along with your wife.

The Fantasy Echo

Miss Merely asked me about "the fantasy echo"
—was she getting it in her poems. "The what?" I said.
"The fantasy echo," she said. "What Doctor Tull
keeps talking about in Post-Rom. Lit." "What is it?"
—"It's sort of, well, how everything in a poem
chimes back to everything else. In "Bud," for instance—
no, this one—'flair and fade' is supposed to echo
'fair and frayed' in line one. Have I got it?"

I saw Joe Tull at lunch. "I'm getting pings
on your 'fantasy echo'" I said, "what the Hell is it?"

"Fantasy echo?—do you mean *fin de siecle?*"

When I saw her on Wednesday I told her, yes, she had it.

I Was Not Sleeping nor Awake

I was not sleeping nor awake. It was
that hour that beaches from the change of sleep:
a touch first, then a shove, and then the wash
of a tide's leaving. Flotsam, still half deep
in the sucked edge that is half sea, half land,
I lay, still blinded, and put out my hand.

It was my hand awoke me. It reached out
and touched where you should be and you were gone.
I sat up, still half nightmared by some thought
the sea had not washed back, half man again
and half a creature still—and you were there
before your mirror, doing up your hair.

I sat back and, a chuckle in my head
the sea has never heard, thought how a priest
might die, and being certain he was dead,
wake to start heaven, and find himself at rest
on nothing, and unwitnessed to that deep.
—Had I been lying out there in my sleep?

my collar turned? my sermon on my cuff?
and all my service canceled to a truth?
Who knows what sleep connects? I'd had enough
of floating edges and the idiot froth
that bubbles out of sleep. I had arrived
back to some manhood. Back to where we lived.

It was a morning of a house in time.
My hand lay empty, but the fact as full
as any made our room as bright a tomb
as heaven is preached. And if its preachers fall
to nothing, why that's nothing. Not to us.
When I woke, all I thought would be there, was.

In Species, Darling

In species, darling, consider how the whale,
a cousin of a sort, once paddled,
as we did yesterday, in summer shallows,

and then went deep. It did not tire, as we did,
of salt that first braced and then stung.
Something called it out and us back,

each to the thing nearest its happiness
as each finds it. I thank you for my kind
against the belittling sea. In idiom

one says, "I love you." Idiom, however,
is the skin of meaning. At whole body depth
we are tropisms, the way each species has

of turning toward some things and away from others.
I turn to you and tremble to a balance.
Or turn and tip to that beam-breaking sea.

Darling

Some have meant only, though curiously,
to believe on evidence. Othello for one.
I suppose he took himself too seriously.
He certainly hadn't much talent for having fun.

No one sets out with intent to become ridiculous.
I used to do push-ups, shower,
read into the lives of the great victorious
and of significant losers. I was sure

something was sure. That there was continuity.
Start with a stone: chip away
whatever is not Apollo—the perpetuity
of Apollo, the locked interplay

of thing and idea—and there you are.
Like Venus from foam, David from a slab
of impossibly cracked Carrara,
soul and its given name even from this flab.

In some sense Commandants
drill time to, this tumescence
of bags and flaps doubling over my pants
is my own doing. But are intentions

nothing? It was done while I wasn't looking,
or looking at something else—at a stone
from which I imagined I was chipping
all that wasn't idea. And down

to gravel too small for anything but bangles,
and too dull for that. I grow, alas,
even-tempered. It is ambition jangles.
We have given and taken mercy. Was

a god locked in the ruined stone? I have come
to a continuity of feeling. It is like leaving
a hung jury and coming home
not guilty, not acquitted, not quite believing

there is a possible verdict, but gladly free.
It is true I made a mess of it. I meant
a shape that eluded me.
I could say I half repent

but that's a dramatic luxury beyond my means,
a handkerchief for Othello. Let us
stay bloodless in love, and not in separate scenes
but in one slow thought gentling to forgiveness.

The Something/Nothing Any Love Can Tell

The something/nothing any love can tell,
but no hate hear, what the sad ghost
of a common thought sighs back to from any hell
that memorizes in black what was almost
enough out of time in its kept green—
that, as I may, I wish us.

                                                    I have seen
no reason to think more can be, nor less.
What is not heaven is a respite we
can be imperfect in, and still let bless
the ghost of what perfections we can see
in some mind's eye, this while a mind and eye
still name the ghost we see our reasons by.

The day long dragbreath of the ghostless trek
through marshes outside love, such as it is,
makes every something nothing. The breakneck
swan dive into a cup at circuses
of angel aerialists gold billboards blare
makes too much of too little. There and there

the trekker ends in quicksand and alone
the diver's act goes wide, once, and no more.
But here, by what can stay out of what is gone,
by what may come that never was before—

not till a mercy stirred—what needs and meets
lets start that something nothing still completes.

What does not wish is dead. What does not guess
all wish may come to nothing wastes its breath.
What treks out its numb-numbered singleness
was born distrustful. And what flings its death
from godstarred perches to the watery eye
of a trick universe, so needs to die

it leaves this life still dreaming. I do not
conclude I love you. I awake and find
I do, and then conclude the little/lot
of loving you is something more than mind
can parse a nothing to. And wish us then
your life and mine, till what we are has been.

A Love Poem

I have labored for her love.
I could not hide my failure.
Nothing could hide my need.

I believe she is grateful.
I bribed her with dances.
A joy still skims.

It makes no difference
except to me. Except
as she is moved to be kind.

I think she is so moved.
We have taken habit of one another.
I can imagine no other mercy.

It is too late for flying lessons.
The bifocal clouds blur.
I am too heavy to skim

what swims before my eyes.
Darling, forgive me,
I can no longer beat time.

Dear Sir

Dear Sir: We haven't met but my father knew you
and spoke of you often, implying an intimacy
on which I perhaps presume. Soon now I too
must make a more formal visit, just as he

knocked, seemingly sure of being received.
I enclose a book I have written. It's mostly questions
he, perhaps, could answer. He once believed
we might communicate. Are there provisions?

If so, would you pass it on to him? If not,
I beg you to forgive the intrusion. We
are uncertain of the protocol. The thought,
whatever the form, is all of courtesy,
and in the hope of hearing from him again.
Till which, with your permission, I remain

etc., and for a while his son
and in some sense I suppose yours also—

John.

Late Peaches

Whatever this is of nature, the peach tree
is in three parts: the trunk and limbs
are a nerve-form in black jade; inside that form,
curled shavings of burnt metal hang in balance,

and among those irid balances the peaches
are a red-buff marzipan. I do not know
what form this is which is equally
sculpture, metal lathe-waste, and boiled sugar,

but these mornings I look out at the peach tree,
and when the mist has dried to diamond points
I see my mother, dried to starch and parchment,
drift from the day like milkweed, pause,

and there, as if she meant to light a candle
inside each peach, stand by the tree and be.

Back

On the mountain after Vesuvius
in what I have left
of the dialect I started from,
I sit with unknown cousins.

Except for the Alfa Romeo
nosing the mayor's house,
a fluorescence of TV reflected
in the glass of an open door,
and the monument to the war dead,
we could choose at a whim
what century we sit to.

We have red wine, bread, *peccorino,*
fave, and garlicky olives before us.
A table set in Pompeii.

Below, at the cliff of San Barbato,
the bearded saint, is the stump
of the Lombard tower my name
came here to in the tenth century,
having crossed the Alps with Alboin
four hundred years earlier
as Gerhardt.

                    I explain
what I have read. They nod respect
that I have read a book.

How he came clanging in 568
allied with Saxons, the conquered
Gedidae sworn to him. Rosamund,
daughter of their murdered king,
his slave queen till 572, when—
all of high Italy under his axe—
she cut his throat to vengeance
for having had a wine bowl
made from her father's skull
and forcing her to drink.

. . . They know the blood of history.
They drink it to fable
and fill the glass again.

A cousin asks, "Was there
a son of that marriage
and was he king after?"

"No. Cleph succeeded.
A chief of another line."

He sips. "It is better so.
But who was Gerhardt?"

. . . An unknown axe-clanger,
the name changed to Gherardi
on his sons' new tongue,
and that to Cerardi
by the time it reached here
some Lombard lordling later,
and again to Ciardi
as, round the mountain
at San Potito Ultra, my fathers
spoke it eight hundred years
till its last sound there
moved to Dover, New Jersey.

They nod. They, too, have names
from these same marches.
Though not my mother—none
she could follow. De Benedictis—
"Of the Blessed"—a church gift
to a foundling at old doors,
its shadow mother
gone to forgotten sorrows, the name
already a thousand year line
in the one furrow it lived from.

On father stones we sit drinking.
The men have bad teeth and loud voices.
Their hands are knobbed
as if by broken knuckles. Haft hands
axed from harder wood than grows here.
The women stand behind us
where the Greeks left them.
When the bottle is empty
they bring another.
                    We talk.
Enough of history. It has been said.
We say nothing. Nothing is necessary.
The wine, the food, the sitting to it
is what there is to say. We say
the wine is good. The *peccorino*
is good. And what olives! Here,
taste this spumanti that I made
myself. Could you buy
a wine like that? Could you?

I am fat, soft-handed,
and have tickets in my pocket—
a choice of oceans.
I am from the miracle
great-uncles left for a century back
leaving them what land there was
to break the knobs of their hands on.

I am of my wristwatch
as they are of sun-up.
                    We talk.
The women the Greeks left
bring us wine and twilight.
Indoors the children watch TV
and the image shimmers
on the glass of an open door.
The mayor's son waves and goes by.
It grows dark.
We sit in whatever century we are left in.
The wine is good. The *peccorino*
is good. The *fave* and the olives
are good.

Echoes

Mother and father knew God and were glad to explain.
I was happy to listen. Love is a conversation.
When I said yes, they agreed, and I agreed.

They touched me when they said. I understood
the touch before the words. There is nothing to argue
in being held closest. Had God been a lion,

I would have done my best to grow a mane,
and to catch lambs to leave dead on His doorstep.
I could catch nothing. I was left to believe.

Love echoes love. I said what I was told
for my pleasure in who told it, for my need
to be held in the telling, apart from true and false.

The conversation is over. Given a choice
between Dante and a stone over two graves,
what shall I read? I have no mother and father.

They have no God unless I remember one
as part of a conversation I forget
except that it pleased me to be touched in the telling.

The Day of the Peonies

This is the day of the peonies. My daughter
in the spell of an abundance that can't last
filled every bowl and vase in the house with water
and mounded the day pink. When I came to breakfast
my transformed toast and coffee were body and blood
of the flowering alter. "The *Times* shall not intrude

on what this is," I read from the introit
and threw it to yesterday. One petal shed
into my cup. "I have my good and know it,"
I acknowledged, a service for the dead;
spooned out the pink omen and drank the waft
of feasted day, half holy and half daft.

For Myra, John L., and Benn

If poets are evidence, let's begin with the fact
that most of ours have been father-bent-and-bound.
If you run to poetic form, I have some contract
to haunt you forty or fifty years beyond
all I can care. But it's you will have to worry
how I behave when I'm out of attention. Sorry.

I hope I don't go boo when you open doors
to closets I'm not in. Not that I'd care,
but I'm moved to now for then. I remember floors
we romped on giggling. You got up from there
lighter, faster, freer. But how can I tell
what you will choose to remember? I know too well

we are already strangers. I am an old
doddering sad-sack with his head in a book
till the book closes on it to all-told
nothing-much. Poor stuff for a real spook,
though you can always sniff the bourbon jug
to summon up a glimpse of the old boy's mug.

If ever I was impressive in your eyes,
and for every time I shouted *no dammit!*
in the finals of self-defense, I apologize.
I hope to slip out the door and not slam it.
I hope I will not rap back with more to say.
I hope I was never too much in your way.

Midnight

He runs in his sleep, snaps, leaps up, without
the rabbit, slipped out of his mouth again. He stands
foolish to the fact. *Where is it?* He lays his snout
across my knee. I show him my spread hands.
I haven't got it. Some of them get away.
He whines—that killer beast. And since I am
God and benevolent, I pay him back
with the last cracker and the bit of ham
left on the plate. Not prey, but at least a snack.
He understands enough theology
to gulp it and curl back to hunt his sleep.
If there are rabbits, that's where they will be.
Who knows? His next kill may be his to keep.

Psalm

I am thinking, Sir, how many conversations
I have invented toward you. They are, in a sense,
scenes from a closet drama. I think about you
in the act of thinking myself, to make sayable
what matters only as it is well said.

Can it be said at all? I have read the psalms.
It is their echoes, not their saying, moves.
It was always so between us. An age of prose
has changed the cadence of echoes, not our intentions.
We mean to sing heaven in place, but lack voice

and are left to drone, not necessarily failures
except as performers. Forgive no, then, bad theater.
I do not even wish a dramatic death.
Let Hamlet have that exit; David the glory
of brass flourishes, the animal audience,

its animal roaring. We must talk it out:
I in some need to think you; you
because I have thought you into this posture of listening.
I invent us to these pictures of one another,
then invent lines as captions. It is called prayer.

It does not describe. It assumes.
It is our habit to take these assumptions seriously.
It is better without dramatics. Truth, if there is
truth, is probably a description of our assumptions.
Consider, Sir: we cannot see the stars

except by assuming pictures, then making the pictures
fix what we see. I invent, for instance, a clock face
around Orion. Sirius is at seven.
Castor and Pollux at ten. Capella at one.
What is the time on a star? What does it matter?

I invent the face of time. At its center, the Belt—
three stars in a row—turns like a little hand broken.
"Three stars in a row," we say. But do stars align?
Alignment is part of the picture we see them in.
I do not impute intention. I am learning to look.

In the simplest lens, for instance, the middle star
becomes a gaseous nebula, revising the picture.
It is an awesome revision; it is as if
our textbooks suddenly spelled realities,
their illustrations almost illustrations.

I am learning to look. I have not learned to see.
I spell you; I cannot say. I begin to guess
those stained-glass portraits that say you to twilight caves
are also pictures for looking at this sky,
this moon is a curved blade, Venus so close

it seems to be inside the suggested circle.
(The Turks, you will remember, made a flag
of this same picture then looked on an empire from it.)
The illusion is both powerful and impossible.
It is also necessary. We do need.

Something. To speak our need. As man, Sir,
his hundred, his two hundred generations
of picture-making has drawn you over and over,
confusing everything but his need to draw
some sort of picture to see with, his hope of seeing.

You have been his vocation. How shall I learn
except by poking through his half-lit lofts—
themselves a heaven of the pictured stars—
to guess what illustrations of himself
he found in training you from dot to dot.

There's that illusion in him. It is both
powerful and impossible. It is pointless,
even for stage purposes, to build it
to a raging climax. Climax is the ruin
of the theatre Oedipus stood in to blind himself.

This is of learning and looking. In time, in drama,
a man may see what he looks at. It will be
himself, his changes, his need to picture his changes.
He will still think of you, perhaps kindly.
When he does see, this conversation must end.

God

I used to be good friends with God, but He
kept playing practical jokes—above all,
when I was sleeping. It is hard to be
easy as friends with someone who can call
Huns from wallpaper roses, or set fire
to brick sidewalks, or leave you without pants
at graduation. Talent is to admire,
but uneasily. You feel you're taking a chance
just saying hello. Well, it's been years now
since we had much to say to one another
and I sleep easier. I don't even know
these nights what my dreams are doing. My mother
used to ask, Do you see Him? And I'd say, I do.
But she's dead. And who is left to lie to?

To Be Delivered on Arrival

I thought to send roses. Masses of roses
white as the heart of light dimmed to a glow.
Roses enough to wait in the room you come to
and make the sufficient place memory owes us.

I have instead sent a check to an agency
that advertises for childhood. Roses, alas,
have turned cannibal. By this agency's guess
the price of a single itemized rose will buy

a season's rice for the scraped bowl. I have added
enough for a gross of bright red bouncing balls.
I give you the light on them, their thunk from the walls
under your window. Once a child is fed

only the reddest ball can bounce as high
as memory must. Come summer again, I promise
all the roses I grow myself. I confess
I have neglected mine. I have heard them cry

for the flesh of children when the bills come due
from the lawn-and-garden shop. Can you suppose
a light you cannot see? Is that no rose?
In any case, this is my last wish to you.

What roses come will be yours if you come or call,
but you won't, and I have stopped gardening. A weed,
sufficiently looked at, does, can, equal in need
all one can bring to the looking, which is all.

It Is for the Waking Man
to Tell His Dreams

sommum
narrare vigiliantis est.
—Seneca

In the stupors before sleep
I used to hear in my head
poems at which God might weep,
each line an angel's bread.

They died awake, their myth
like the gold plates, God-bright,
Moroni brought to Smith
and then took back each night.

I wired my bed and taped
those oracles. Come day,
I heard: "The cat escaped
when Jesus ran away

with Mary's lamb, no doubt."
—And then a snore,
until the tape ran out,
the dog scratched at the door,

hearing its master's voice.
It is a dog's mistake
to wagtail and rejoice
because the fool's awake.

The Aging Lovers

Why would they want one another,
those two old crocks of habit
up heavy from the stale bed?

Because we are not visible where we dance,
though a word none hears can call us
to the persuasion of kindness, and there sing.

Sounds

Sin for my Master's sake
whispers the Snake.

Carve me erect on Zion
roars the black Lion.

Repent for what I am
quavers the bloody Lamb.

I am for love, for love,
mourns the soft Dove.

Mankind will keep me fat
chitters the sitting Rat.

I'll always be around
whimpers the Hound.

Not if my tusks can gore
grunts the sharp Boar.

(I had a dream I can
hardly explain, says Man.)

A Trenta-Sei of the Pleasure
We Take in the Early Death of Keats

It is old school custom to pretend to be sad
when we think about the early death of Keats.
The species-truth of the matter is we are glad.
Psilanthropic among exegetes,
I am so moved that when the plate comes by
I almost think to pay the god—but why?

When we think about the early death of Keats
we are glad to be spared the bother of dying ourselves.
His poems are a candy store of bitter-sweets.
We munch whole flights of angels from his shelves
drooling a sticky glut, almost enough
to sicken us. But what delicious stuff!

The species-truth of the matter is we are glad
to have a death to munch on. Truth to tell,
we are also glad to pretend it makes us sad.
When it comes to dying, Keats did it so well
we thrill to the performance. Safely here,
this side of the fallen curtain, we stand and cheer.

Psilanthropic among the exegetes,
as once in a miles-high turret spitting flame,
I watched boys flower through orange winding sheets
and shammed a mourning because it put a name
to a death I might have taken—which in a way
made me immortal for another day—

I was so moved that when the plate came by
I had my dollar in hand to give to death
but changed to a penny—enough for the old guy,
and almost enough saved to sweeten my breath
with a toast I will pledge to the Ape of the Divine
in thanks for every death that spares me mine.

I almost thought of paying the god—but why?
Had the boy lived, he might have grown as dull
as Tennyson. Far better, I say, to die
and leave us a formed feeling. O beautiful,
pale, dying poet, fading as soft as rhyme,
the saddest music keeps the sweetest time.

38

Sitting Bull at the Circus

The treaty broken again, the lands lost,
the children of the Sioux eat government maggots
from the infected hand of the Great White Father,
the braves grown old, sour in their own skins
in the stink and sweat of defeat, in the blown nations
of the sands and water scarce even to dig for
and palm to the mouth dirty—Sitting Bull
in the feathers, paint, and totem of his fathers
went East to a roaring circus to be looked at
and look at Buffalo Bill who looked so much
like Yellow Hair, his name above the dead
at the bend of the Little Big Horn, that last day
of power for the Nations, he seemed a spirit;
and think, what medicine can hold back
the day of the ghost, the scalp of the Yellow Flag
waving from the lodge pole, no longer dead
but turned white and returned to the dancing horse
of spectacle—himself a spectacle
down from the ridge top where his raised arm
called down the nations, their last day
to strike and see the dead get up as ghosts,
the dancing horses of the dancing men
whose heads were flags, driving the buffalo
through dust to dust, and no day left to come.

Obit

After he retired, for something to do
he took up high-stakes gin, an exercise
in pure chance where always the same few
winners chance in and out. The surprise
is he didn't break sooner. At sixty-nine
he started a new business, an end-of-the-line,

make-it-or-go-on welfare venture. But there
he knew what he was doing. At seventy-four
he sold out to Conglomerate Money to Spare
for seven million and stock and once more
was looking for something to do and tried
collecting stamps but it bored him and he died.

His children were grateful. His widow, who had feared
they would have to sell the house and take a flat,
memorialized him with a tomb they shared
after twenty-three years of finding out
it doesn't matter how much you get through
day after day when there is nothing to do.

An Overthrow

Under the cottonwoods
by the iron bridge
the dead man lay to summer,
his mouth
a bomb of flies,
his eyes the color of meat
in a face faintly iris
through a film
dust-gray as pigeon wings.

Fred Armbuster was with me.
"Ned Forey!" he said.
"We'll have to remember exactly
how we found him
and how he looked
and we'd best touch nothing
till the sheriff comes."
And because it was necessary
I remembered exactly.
But the coroner
certified natural causes
and I was not asked.
It was no longer
exactly necessary.

But when I was twenty-three
on this same grass
under the cottonwoods
Ned Forey's Ava and I
rolled naked as fish
one summer night.
I remember her
taken and warm, her thighs,
like a nest for moonlight.
I forget her eyes.
I could not see her eyes.
But her flesh went down
from breast to ribs to belly
in three falls
the color of moon and honey.

And for these reasons
I know this place exactly.
Ned's gone from it, and Ava
is married in San Diego, and I
walk past it with my daughter,
wishing her moonlight.

Matins

It froze in Paris last night and a rag doll
that had been a woman too tattered-old to notice
turned up stiff on a bench. So the police,
who spend least on the living, paid to haul
nothing to nothing. She could have lived for a week
on what the bureau will spend on paper work;

for a year in the sun on the autopsy fees,
filing, storage, crating, and putting down.
What keeps us wrong? Dolls cannot walk around
all night on shredded legs. And in a freeze
everyone else walks faster. Dolls need to rest,
then can't get up again. It may be best

when there's nowhere to go, to fall asleep and be there.
I have only the *Times* item of squeezed prose.
It was a cable in by night-rate, I suppose,
when everything's cheapest and easiest to bear
deepest under and a sea across
to my breakfast table, still anonymous.

But told. And not to nothing. Every child
risked from love and held must be put down
to walk itself away, and turn by turn
become another. This dirty doll unheld
by any arm is the one altar piece
from which mad Francis learned to be a priest.

gy for a Cove Full of Bones

—Saipan: Dec. 16, '44

Tibia, tarsal, skull, and shin:
Bones come out where the guns go in.
Hermit crabs like fleas in armor
Crawl the coral-pock, a tremor
Moves the sea, and surf falls cold
On coves where glutton rats grow bold.
In the brine of sea and weather
Shredded flesh transforms to leather,
And the wind and sea invade
The rock-smudge that the flame throwers made.

Death is lastly a debris
Folding on the folding sea:
Blankets, boxes, belts, and bones,
And a jelly on the stones.
What the body taught the mind
Flies explore and do not find.
Here the certain stood to die
Passionately to prove a lie.
At the end a covenant's pall
Of stones made solid, palpable,
Moves the victory to the sea,
And the wind indifferently.
Hate is nothing, pity less.
Angers lead us to digress:
I shall murder if I can,
Spill the jellies of a man.

Or be luckless and be spilled
In the wreck of those killed.

Nothing modifies our end:
Nothing in the ruin will mend.
If I moralize, forgive:
Error is the day we live.
In the ammoniac coves of death
I am choked for living breath.
I am tired of thinking guns,
Knowing where the bullet runs.
I am dreaming of a kiss
And a flesh more whole than this.
I am pondering a root
To destroy the cove-rat's loot.
I am measuring a place
For the living's living grace.
I am running from the breath
Of the vaporing coves of death.
I have seen our failure in
Tibia, tarsal, skull, and shin.

Thinking about Girls

All day I have been thinking about girls.
All the girls I have really thought about,
my daughter excepted, are grandmothers now.

This morning at half-past-nothing on Delauncy
I met a grandmother I had thought about once
as something else—because she was something else.

We said our surprises and had a cup of espresso.
She asked for Sanka but they didn't have it.
"It will keep me awake forever," she said. Some cups

do that, but must be drunk. We sat and drank.
I stared at her wrinkles that had wrinkles in them.
She stared at my flab as if to find me in it.

We kept trying to remember. Then looked again
with no cause to remember, but only to see
there was more ruin than there had been Rome.

The stones multiply in dividing to nothing.
I sat in the enlarged city and watched the young
dance by us on Delauncy in plate-glass time.

A single blink froze us a millennium dead.
I studied us one instant from my own death.
Then left some money, kissed a ghost we know,

a dryest peck, then blinked it off in a taxi
to a street below two temples one on the other.
Then back to today in which I thought about girls.
Which came to nothing really. Where it began.

An Old Man Confesses

I have no cause, and God has not confessed
what purpose time serves. I am bored by death.
I have its cave-damp glowing in my chest.
I have its stone-dust muddied on my breath.

Carrion. Age is carrion. I disgust
even the flesh I am. And where's the priest
so clean of bloat, so justified and just
he could strip back such skins and find a feast?

Get him away, half-woman as he is
and smelling of old cupboards. I am gone
into a mud deeper than the abyss
down which his adolescent angels shone

like energies. Ah, what a world that was!
I could have leaped to Heaven on my own legs!
Now bats hang from the rafters of the house
and blow-flies bore my flaps to lay their eggs.

Only my tongue stays fast. Rattle and clatter.
As if it signified to say and say.
Maybe saying it is the heart of the matter.
Or just that it costs so little to prattle away.

Say the old fool went prattling to the end.
All words taste better than the gas I sigh.
And while words last me, I can still pretend
that I may phrase some reason not to die.

I doubt it. Let these words do: "The old sot
lay at his last gasp in a rotten hide
and ran words like a leakage, till the rot
inside the fact had drained. And then he died."

Caught as We Are

Caught as we all are in the human condition—
Subject to vices variously begun—
in curiosity, from nature, or malaise.
Hungry for joy and fed less than our hunger.
Charitable when we can save ourselves
from more involvement than we know how to bear.
Simple in our silences, made intricate by vocabularies.
Greedy because we were all once children.
Forgoing because we have read dreams and visions
that do not come to us when we lay the book by.
Loving in desperation, in fear of loneliness.
Begetting in the arsons and Olympics of first love
or in the habituated rutting of the long bed
the children that sadden us to an uneasy tolerance.
Afraid of death in our dying and liberated
only partially by the partial loss of ignorance.
Eager for friendships from which we may demand
what we ourselves give with two motives, if at all.
Suspected by States for our best intuitions.
Solemn at funerals but glad to have outlived
one other as proof that we are, after all, right.
Liars because we must live in what seems possible.
Fools because we lie, and fools again for assuming
the possible to be any more likely than the impossible.
Faithless because our houses are destroyable but not our
    fears.

Brave because we dare not stop to think. Proud
because we are wrong. Wrathful because we are powerless.
Envious because we are uncertain. Lazy because we
    were born.
Avaricious because we are afraid. Gluttonous
because bellies are a mother to warm and assure us.
Murderous and adulterous because opportunity and energy
will sometimes be added to motive. Ungrateful
because gratitude is a debt, and because it is easier
to betray our benefactors than to await new benefactions.
Religious because it is dark at night, and because
we have been instructed, and because it is easier to obey
than to believe our senses or to learn to doubt them
exhaustively. Sad because we are as we are,
time-trapped, and because our images of ourselves
and the facts of ourselves wake at night and bicker
and lay bets with one another, with us as the stakes.

Then moved to pity at last because we hear and are
    saddened—
Nearly beautiful in the occasions of our pity not of
ourselves. Nearly affectionate when we are free of pain.

Caught as we are in these and our other conditions—
   Which include a distaste for the littleness of our motives,
   and, therefore, some wish to live toward some reality.
   Terrified by realities. Addicted to evasions. Daring, perhaps
   once, to look into the mirror and see and not look away.

Beginning again, then, with those who share with us and
      with whom
   we share the sorrows of the common failure.
   Fumbling at last to the language of a sympathy
   that can describe, and that will be, we are persuaded,
   sufficiently joy when we find in one another its idioms.

Caught as we are in these defining conditions—
   I wish us the one fact of ourselves that is inexhaustible
   and which, therefore, we need not horde nor begrudge.
   Let mercy be its name till its name be found.
   And wish that to the mercy that is possible because it takes
   nothing from us and may, therefore, be given indifferently,
   there be joined the mercy that adds us to one another.

A Traffic Victim Sends a Sonnet of Confused Thanks to God as the Sovereign Host

Please do not think of me as a surly guest.
I ate, drank, read, roamed, romped in a few
of your lavish oceans. I suspect you knew
I was bouncing your daughters—may they be ever blest!
Then, suddenly, crossing the street, I was under arrest!
I can hardly believe it. Nor can I get through:
not one phone call. I have tried to thank you;
my prayers keep coming back to me misaddressed.
I feel my case has been blown out of all proportion.
Tomorrow I am being taken to death row.
For jaywalking! Law is its own contortion.
It insists on holding me incommunicado.
But I'm still free to scratch a thanks on the wall
To say you host a sweet world, all in all.

On Something Like the
Temptation of St. Anthony

The devil that came closest was all sincerity.
"Unless it is useful," he said, "I never lie.
Even then I prefer, as a matter of personal style,
to piece the truth. My sin, as you know, is pride;
my hobby honesty. I am weary of it
and weary of myself, and want nothing
but the obliteration of defeat.
Being proud, however, I refuse to fall
in a minor skirmish. If there is a main thrust in you
I am prepared to meet it and go under
in admiration of splendor."

                              . . . You may yourself
meet him. He did not fall to me. Did I
to him? I told him he was diluting
the quality of my attention. "How?" he asked.
"With platitudes," I told him. He half bowed:
"Let me be bold: what could I bribe you with?"
"With worms," I said, "if I were first disgusted
with all of any day." He bowed a full bow.
"I may be back," he said. And he may be back.

A Successful Species

Horseshoe crabs, which are not crabs at all
but hardshell salt-marsh spiders, made their way
under the froth-edge of the littoral
and back to the marsh precisely on the day
and night and noon of the animal flood tide.
The females puddle their eggs and males ride

over the pools in clouds of sperm. They are
a successful species. In part, perhaps, because
they are food for nothing in particular.
For nothing, in fact, till they die and decompose
into the generalized stock of the salt broth
fans and tendrils reach for under the froth.

Success of species, as it is understood
by species watchers, is measured by how long
they manage to come ashore timed to the flood
of their breeding stew. The flight continues; the wrong
leak back into the salt soup, whereat
they fail their tidal appointment and that's that.

Our colonial founders, who may have seen straighter,
called it the horsefoot crab but could not explain
its boney tail which, as discovered later,
is mostly for turning upright once again
when a gust of surf flips it half-defenseless
onto its back. Nothing in nature is senseless.

Except perhaps what thinks to scriptualize
what it has lost adaption to; for instance,
this creature's infallible timer. We surmise.
It is. And seems prepared to go the distance.
To nowhere in particular, to be sure.
But the one success of species is to endure.

Ten Minutes My Captive

A turtle, rattlesnake-backed but horny
and slowed from striking because he
is defended as soon as he shuts; a cousin
of venom but not venomous, and of Sin
but no tempter; reptile
from the egg but watered to a style
of its own, then land-bound again; a between;
a three-tracked trail in sand, a stone
in dust, a mossback on wet logs;
then an oyster with six legs
waving under the wavering mercury sky
of the swimming hole where I,
in the impulse of a dive, passing it, snatched,
came ashore with it, and watched
ten minutes of a mystery, queer as any,
cower dead in its box, then stir, then plainly
unbud a head, unbead two eyes, sway
a Lazarus look at the world, find legs, and crawl away
like half an immortality, safe in its tomb,
into the green flecked edge of water and home.

Sea-Birds

Sea-birds on a windy carousel
spun spinning holidays offshore
one of the days the world went well.

The battleship *Potemkin* wore
a flag of weather at its top.
It passed those birds and passed no more.

The *Big Mo* had no time to stop.
It pushed the weather to the East
and there its shells began to drop.

The wolfpack's commodore had at least
his own skin to think about
and once torpedoes were released

he dove and could not look out
to see the sea-birds' holiday.
Given the facts, there's room to doubt

he would have seen them, anyway.
And when the depth charge made a mess
of all the tricks in which he lay

the sea-birds, full of this success
at being happy in the blow,
beyond perfection or distress
never saw the navies go.

In the Audience

A sparrow lights on wisteria,
jitters like a wind-up toy,
spins feathery propellers,
blurs off.
        Last night June bugs
flew bomber missions, crashing
against the porch screens
as I sat reading.
        This morning
I went crabbing, and one
that fell out of the pail
crossed the sand like a dismembered
magician's hand limbering.
I could have caught it back
but there was more to see
than have. It closed its fist
on sea-lace and disappeared. What
a good act!
        There is this
world I go to. Everything's
in it. I watch changes,
waiting for what things
turn out to be, not always
good, but there, and always
changing.
        I shall be sorry
when the show is over.

Napping by the Fence

A green-drooled cow all rumpled suede
looked over a rail. A bird perched on one horn,
preened itself, separate as it was born,
then separated again. The cow stayed
grinding inside itself, then tossed its head,
birdless, and swung away, not so much gone
as preoccupied. So that much had been done
of perhaps as much as one minute of one day
I happened into with no intention to stay.

Nine Gray Geese

I saw nine gray geese flying by
    Like three ghosts down Fifth Avenue
Just about thirty stories high
    As I looked down from thirty-two!

I had stayed with my Uncle Mark.
    He lives in what he calls a "suite"
That looks out over Central Park
    Just north of 62nd St.

I woke up early, I recall
    And went out on his balcony.
Central Park was dressed for Fall.
    A salt breeze blew in from the sea.

The first light seemed to rise like steam.
    Traffic below me moved like toys.
It was silent as a dream.
    Then suddenly I heard a noise:

Honk!—just once—and nine gray geese
    Skimmed by—below me!—on their way
To where ghosts go in chains of V's
    From Canada to Paraguay.

All I saw of them was their backs.
    Just for a blink. Then they were gone.

South of the Plaza, out past Saks,
　　　Across the harbor and the dawn

To anywhere! That's what it is
　　　To be a goose. Then suddenly
I smelled toast and heard bacon sizz
　　　And I went back to being me,

Which starts with breakfast! But I knew
　　　A single glimpse is all we get
Of ghostly gray geese flying through,
　　　And that we never can forget.

The sun will sink and the sun will rise
　　　Day by day the same. And then
There comes a moment of surprise
　　　And everything is new again!

This Moving Meaninglessness

It is, I think, a robin tinkling away
in the hemlock shade of noon heat.
It is not much song. Listless as the day
it slurs three, and repeat, three and repeat.

The grass needs cutting. The day lies flung in a shade,
half into the ground. The tinkling skips a beat
then stops. Has all of it been played?
It was not much song but may it repeat and repeat.

March 20, 1970

It snowed too thin to fall
    or, falling, leave a trace.
Air snow. Pure interval.
    Condition without place.

A non-result, non-cause.
    A coming not to come.
An almost never-was.
    Not to. Not from.

But changing all between,
    nothing above, below.
Transparencies of a scene.
    It snowed the ghost of snow.

December 13, 1979

Three squirrels wound and sprung to this remitted
December day chase tumble tails on the lawn.
They must be winter-sure in the elm, permitted
by a plenty in its boles. There's not one acorn
on or under the oak. They go to go.
But why this lawn party? I think they know

the dog is old and stiff, his monster slacked.
His ears tense toward them but it takes four
deliberate heaves to get his hind legs cocked
as if to spring. And what shall he spring for?
There is no energy after energy.
He quivers feral, but then looks at me

as if I might serve them to him in a dish
like Greeks godsent to the ogre. Of my guilt
that I have uncreatured a world to this mish-mash
whine and quiver half-down in the silt
of a sludged instinct, I toss him a soy bone.
He settles for my bogus and settles down.

And the squirrels spin, almost as if they flew,
to the top of the split shake fence, into the spruce,
across it over the roof, over the yew
and into the hemlock thicket, fast and loose,
as fast as easy, around and around again
in the feast of being able to. Amen.